The Traces of Song

First published in 2005 by
St. John's College Research Centre
Oxford OX1 3JP, UK

© 2005 St. John's College Research Centre

Printed in Great Britain by
Information Press

ISBN   0 9544975 5 4

The Traces of Song
Selections from Ancient Arabic Poetry

Translated with an introduction by
Walid Khazendar

Calligraphic paintings by
Mouneer al-Shaarani

St. John's College Research Centre

Some of these translations have been published as separate leaflets in St. John's College Research Centre, Oxford. The translations: *They have shot me*; *The veil dropped*; *I have drunk the wine*; *Sways with her trinkets* were presented in a public poetry reading at St. John's College, Oxford, on 25th February 2003, and the translations: *Is it for the ruins*; *I spend the night*; *When will the tormented* were presented on a similar occasion on 27th November 2003. As regards this volume I am grateful to the poet Walid al-Halis, for his comments and suggestions. I am also grateful to Robin Ostle, my colleague at St. John's College, without whose constant support it would have been difficult to complete this book.

Contents

Introduction

In selecting and translating these short poems and extracts from ancient Arabic poetry I have sided with the inner voice of the poem or the poet, and I have tried to render the whole of this voice with its tones and overtones. The translations, consequently, deal with poetry as a personal experience of the poet and as his life, but as he saw and felt it, and reacted to it. They do not deal with poetry as a reflection of the poet's historical and social conditions. For poetry, when it is poetry, is not a mere reflection or echo of any factor outside it; it is a creative, artistic vision that surpasses its factual considerations. The artistic work, especially when it is creative, does not reflect or describe its material, but it reshapes and recreates it in every impulse of the imagination, according to how the artist sees and feels it. Michelangelo, while working on a piece of stone with his chisel, was searching, as he once said, for the body which he saw from the very beginning, sleeping in the stone. While he was sculpting he was awakening and freeing this body. Reshaping is the essence of art, and this is why we need it. It is an action of a deep and crucial emancipation, an action of unchaining, not of bearing the chains. And poetry is a profound sculpture of reality, and it changes reality and reshapes it according to how it sees this reality, using its most sharp and dangerous chisel: language.

Poetry, including ancient Arabic poetry, is not 'a mirror that reflects …' and so forth; it is, rather, the vision that takes reality into its own dimension, promoting it to the level of art that belongs to everybody, to every place and to every time. If poetry is obliged to be a 'mirror', it will not be that sleek, smooth, and cold mirror which is very dark on one side to 'reflect' in the other, but it will be that magic and profound mirror, without any dark side, which leads to the endless interactive depth of the human, language and being. You can see the historical and the social there, if you insist, but they are vague, dreamy, evasive and uncertain. The more you follow them, the more you will be misled and the more you will mislead those who follow you.

My aim is to make it clear that the translation, or study, which deals with ancient Arabic poetry, or any poetry, as a historical or social document, is reducing poetry to a mere smooth and cold surface, quite outside its linguistic, poetic and imaginative dimension and charge. All translations, or studies, that focus on 'furniture in ancient Arabic poetry', for example, or on 'clothes', 'food', 'plants', 'wine', 'women', 'woman's body', 'women's rights', 'sex', and so on, are not literary translations or studies. I don't say that these works are bad or that we don't need them, for they may be of value, and sometimes we may need them. I say only that such works do not belong to literature, but to other fields of scientific, socio-historical knowledge: carpentry, fashion, dietetics, dendrology, oenology, anatomy, sociology, sexology and so forth. What specifies the kind of translation or study is not the kind of document under consideration, but the kind of reading of this document, how we read it and why.

I would also argue that socio-historical translations and studies of the kind mentioned above not only reduce ancient Arabic poetry to mere lists of facts, to a kind of tourist guide of the Arabian peninsula in the fifth century A.D., but they are misleading even at the level of their own socio-historical fields. On the one hand, such translations and studies have to be done by specialists in these fields because only they are qualified to read the document, any document, historically and socially, in a proper methodological and scientific manner. On the other hand, the ancient Arab poet, in particular, and perhaps every poet, did not speak of objects or make connections between them in a way that allows us to conceptualise or analyse them as realistic, socio-historical facts. He spoke of things around him as he saw them and as he felt them, not as they are in reality. Moreover, poetry does not emerge only from what is there, but from what could have been there; not only from what already happened, but from what could have happened.

The translation or study of poetry means to translate or study the poem itself, and not to use it. The challenge and the target and the virtue here lie in transforming the language of the poem itself, and how this language worked to create or recreate the meaning. What matters is not the object as it is, but its linguistic presence; not the motif as such, but its poetic and aesthetic charge which language carries; not only the ghost of meaning, but also its structure.

◊

From the monsoon climate of the Indian Ocean in the south, to the Syrian desert in the north, and from Mesopotamia in the east to the Red Sea and further to the river Nile in the west, such was the stage of ancient Arabic poetry at the dawn of history. Its scenery, over such a huge area, at such an early time, was remarkably changeable and unpredictable: from the height of summer hotness and the simoom wind, to the extreme of winter coldness with its rain and frost; vast desert and high mountains, cliffs and caves, one wilderness after the other, a sudden oasis, or an unexpected fierce and hungry beast. The dramatic and crucial question was to resist or to perish.

And somehow there was a gap in history, like those many gaps in dreams, or the many forgotten moments in intoxication. Then history awoke, swaying with a new language, with gifted poets and passionate lovers. We know nothing of this poetry before the first poems of 'Amr ibn Qami'a (5th-6th cent. A.D.), or the complete first ode of Imru' al-Qays (6th cent. A.D.), in spite of the advanced artistic features apparent in their poetry, and their astonishing images. What we do know is that from the fifth century A.D. at least, under an ambiguous sky and in a ruthless land, one of the most important poetic experiences had begun to share, with the poetic experiences of other human beings, the early formulation of the basic questions of language and being: language was beckoning, becoming, and Man was perceiving linguistically the features of his being.

◊

Place is a major and integral dimension of the ancient Arabic poem, and so often it is the backbone of its structure. Time in this poetry is present and concentrated emotionally, and hence semantically, in or around a specific place. The poem does not emerge from nowhere, or proceed to nowhere. It is either in a place or coming from a place or going to a place. *Is the whole of time alighting and departing?*, cries the ancient Arab poet al-Muthaqqib al-'Abdi. Transience is the principal feature of place in the ancient poem, and absence is her dominant theme. Every place has either vanished or is waiting for its inevitable fate of destruction. This is what haunted 'Alqama al-Fahl:

Every home, even if it lasts long
On its supports, will inevitably be destroyed

The poet was in a very critical state, living always between the place and its imminent destruction. Presence and absence were always the twins casting his being back and forth, and, as Abu al-'Atahiya shows, he sometimes did not know the former from the latter:

You had fun, and you took many lessons
As if you were absent from them, while you were present

Or al-Sanawbari, who says:

Homes of the loved ones, which are not homes,
I see you as homes of the present absent.

This painful sense of Place is not restricted to his *loved ones'* home but it extends to, and dwells in, every place: the fountainhead, the pasture, the childhood playground, places of amusement and everywhere around him.

But let us linger here a little, for the deserted, ruined home of the loved ones, or the beloved, is one of the most emotional themes of ancient Arabic poetry. It was both the absence of the beloved and the remnants of her presence at one and the same time. For the ancient poet, the home is a place only because it contains people, only because it achieves its glorious deed of 'placing'. Because of this, homes are not only made from stones, but from the presence, breaths and souls of their dwellers. 'Antara ibn Shaddad says:

Home, the spirits of homes are their inhabitants
If they depart, bodies will weep over them

There is no emptiness in the language and poetic sphere of the ancient Arab poet, and if this emptiness happens in reality, the poet loses his linguistic-ontological balance. His poem was still a child, and the thing and its naming were the two legs of one stride, they were one object in reality and one impulse in language. Hence, the collapse of objects in reality unsettles and threatens to undermine their names in language and their perceptual integrity. The beloved's home when it becomes a ruin and her presence when it becomes absence are also the ruin and absence of their proper names in language. And the poet has to confront this loss, and has to try and restore the unity and regain the balance. He, or his poem, has to rebuild what has been destroyed by appealing, calling and naming, and sometimes he asks for a response. 'Antara ibn Shaddad stood, yet again, in front the rubble of his beloved home:

'Abla's home, in Jiwa', speak!
And have a good morning, 'Abla's home, and be safe.

'Abla is the name of his beloved, and *Jiwa'* is the place name of her home.

The counterpart of the contradictory presence/absence is the interactive place/dweller. Hence, the traces of the vanished home are the traces of the beloved, by which the song can trace, invoke and restore her. But here we should pause and begin from a different, reflective and unconditional point of departure. From this point on, we will see how the ancient Arabic poem, or song, will begin to sculpt its model, exactly like Michelangelo. It will emancipate the beloved and the place from reality and reshape them as it wanted and needed to see them. It is impossible, for example, to find that 'perfect in everything' beloved anywhere beyond the poem, either in the Arabian peninsula or in any other place in the world. For she is not only a woman, but she is a revenge against Time and Fate: the absolute equivalent of an uncompensated and insufferable loss. The poem is the poet's rebelling against his reality through carrying and reshaping its burden, through turning the abyss of absence downside up, rather than looking down into the abyss in panic.

◊

There are at least three different functions of Time in the ancient Arabic poem: two are subsidiary, of which the first is Time as 'Witness', and the second is Time as 'Friend'; then there is the dominant Time which is Time as 'Fate'. These three functions or kinds of time are not connected in the poem; each occurs alone and has its specific task.

The time of mingling and getting close has gone
And this one is the time of separating and excluding

al-Sharif al-Radi

Time as Witness has the task of passing, parallel to the poet's life,

12

and of recording the poet's days and acts. *Time is a string of events and matters* as al-Buhturi says. It is Time during which the poet will not do something bad or will continue doing something good:

I swore I will not satirise all through time except those who satirised me

Ibn al-Rumi

And:

By your life, hunger bit me once
Then I swore I would not deprive any hungry one all through time

Ghaniya bint 'Afif

And this time is a witness which is always ready to testify to the poet's deeds and sometimes it recites the poet's poems, as al-Mutanabbi says:

Time is only one of the transmitters of my necklaces,
When I utter poetry time becomes a reciter

And this time is mostly honest, tolerant and not racist:

Time did not disgrace my colour
Nor did the blackness degrade my high stature

'Antara ibn Shaddad

But if this kind of time does not fulfil its function of testifying to the poet's deeds, it will be relegated to its reality, to being merely Time passing:

Is time anything but today or yesterday or tomorrow?
This is how time between us comes and goes

Hatim al-Ta'i

So, Time just comes and goes, unemployed. And:

Is time anything but a night and its day,
But the sunrise and sunset?

Abu Dhu'ayb al-Hudhali

Time as Friend is the weakest one; it does not appear much in the poem and many times the poet had to defend it:

For my sake and respect, do not abuse time wrongly, for it is my friend

Abu Tammam

It is a secret time, a mostly nocturnal accompanying of the poet: It *stays, as I want, at my side*, as al-Sahib ibn 'Abbad said. It is a secret time because it allows and also attends the poet's pleasure, stealthily, out of sight of both the first kind of time (because this time is the witness of the poet's deeds only) and out of sight of the third kind of time (which is the enemy of the poet).

It is also a laughing Time:

Time is laughing from the cheerfulness of his joy
And life is becoming dewy from the freshness of his body

al-Buhturi

And this time drinks wine, and sometimes it is this time which becomes *drunk*, not the poet:

As to my telling how I spent my night
It's that I found time drunk, overfull

Ibn Ghalbun al-Suri

Time as Fate is inimical time. For it comes, suddenly, as mentioned before, with death and destruction, and especially, to intervene and stop the work of the other two kinds of time. And unlike Place, this time is the intruder in the poem, and not intertwined with it. It does not witness or attend anything which may be good for the poet. And it does not emerge in or from the poem but it is, mostly, the enemy that completed its destructive work before the poem, or it is expected to do so thereafter. It does not work in the poem, but its enmity appears in it, as a consequence, in the ruins, or as an expectation in its language that is haunted with absence. This kind of time is immoral: it is unjust, ruthless and sometimes treacherous, as al-Nabigha al-Ja'di said:

Don't trust treacherous time, for
Anyhow it is fickle with people

This time is mean and stingy. Rarely does it give anything good, and even then it takes it back:

When time took back from me its gift
And the ravines of love began to split open again
I stayed with separation, weeping over it, regretting
And asking it, how could the past return?

Mihyar al-Daylami

And the poet sometimes steals pleasure through this kind of time, but while it is sleeping, as al-Tha'alibi says:

Time slept, then we noticed and we stole
A portion of pure pleasure

This is why, perhaps, the poem usually breaks out after or before the occurrence of Time as Fate. The poem emerges after this occurrence to rebuild linguistically, restore and resurrect, and hence, contrary to Time, the present of the poem is the past. And the poem emerges before the occurrence of this time in order to precede it, to predict, preparing itself to confront it as the enemy that carries death and destruction. And here is the other side of the ordeal, when the present of the poem, in the face of Time, is the future; when what is not happening now in the present is happening, ahead, in the future. What I have said just now may appear for the English reader difficult to achieve in a poem, but this is one of the most important poetic potentials of the ancient Arabic poem. And this potential is taken from the Arabic language itself, for the verb in the present tense in Arabic—because of its inimical relationship with Time—can also mean the past and the future.

◊

The overwhelming sense of Place and its opponent, Time, is the dominant trait of the ancient Arabic poem that permeates all its themes. Everything in this poem is experienced, imagined and poetised through the tension of this feeling: the beloved, the home, the foe, the praised one, the satirised one …., all are gauged and viewed poetically through the dualistic measure of Place/Time. This is why the poem, in my view, is one solid unit. It is a poem that is brimful with life as we have seen, full of concrete images and lyrical, personal tones, moving from one theme to another impetuously and without 'preamble'; without claiming any logical connections. For its unity is deeper than this and does not need any powerless logical connectives.

There has been much debate about the form of the ancient Arabic poem. Most of the participants have accused this poem of being disassembled and without that unity renowned as 'organic'. There were few who tried to see 'its' unity, or who did not focus only on the ready-made critical unity which the former insist on imposing upon the poem. I will not participate in this argument now. I would like, instead, to give some space to what ancient Arab poets themselves have said about their poems:

It is poetry like the blossoms of the orchard which I harmonised
With a speech that makes poetry, however difficult, easy

Bashshar ibn Burd

If I pass away I will leave behind me
Rhymes that please the quoters
Their stanzas are pleasant and well-knit
If poetry could be worn they would be clothed

Ibn Mayyada

If poetry has no stature in your view

15

While it is like the pearls of speech of a speaker
And while it is right and truthful, without fault
Save that it is built like houses are built

....

al-Ahwas al-Ansari

In their own words the ancient Arab poets considered their poem to be harmonised like the flowers in the orchard, well-knit like a woven fabric and built like a house. The ancient Arabic poem has nothing to do with the 'organic'. It does not grow or spread like plants but it moves ahead, always making more connections. It is a structural interaction, not an 'organic unity'. It is many flowers harmonised in one *orchard*, or it is built stone by stone as a room, and room by room, to form one *house*, and between this and that it is *well-knit* to the extent that you could *wear* it as a dress, *if poetry could be worn*. The mind that is preoccupied by the 'organic' dimension or unity is unlikely to find anything to satisfy it in the form of this poem. And quite apart from the ancient Arabic poem, the 'organic' concept may be very important in biology, but I do not think it has any value in poetics. There is no 'organic' poem at any time or place, just as we cannot find, in any time or place, a structural potato or carrot.

◊

The ancient Arab poet, as he appears in his poem, is passionate, rebelling against Time, always travelling, and worried about Fate. But he is also generous, and has a moral message; he is tolerant of his tribe and friends and very tender with his beloved. And amidst all this he is a cheerful pessimist, sad-full-of-hope, impetuous-wise, all in one. Thus his poem is a poem of motion and surging; emotional, extravagant and not conceptual, in the sense that it is intuitive and not philosophical. This poem meditates deeply but sensuously with its body, I mean its language, hugging life and not separated from it. This is a poem without ready-made feelings and emotions, but rather with feelings and emotions which flare up suddenly here and there, all through its verses. For a poem like this, language had to be a language of naming and not referring, of calling and not coding, of singing and imagining, and not listing and analysing. It does not report life, but falls upon it.

When this poem sets out on its journey through the desert, it sets out at the same moment on its own eager quest for domination over all that it sees and feels. It exposes its poet, vehemently, clearly without any falsehood, in order to expose his weakness in the face of Time, his fears of Fate and his disappointments in love. It does this in order to free him from them all, to prepare him to face, bravely and poetically the terrible venture of his journey through the brutality of Time, the remains of Place and the impossibility of love. With its poet, the poem ventures verse by step from one wilderness to another, passing perils and animals, under a scorching sun in a wasteland, while the severity of the desert night waits for them:

16

How many a wilderness—as if,
When the wind strikes it, it is threadbare fragments,
The reckless wind dies in its spaces
And every spring decays in its territories—
Have I crossed, in vain, on a light mount, as if its saddle
Is on an ostrich, climbing the two mountains of Agharr, startled
As if the two pillars of its body that trembled with it,
With their two fore parts, are burning Ben tree branches.
It worries about its eggs as the night has approached,
And the rain penetrates a dripping, moist nest

Muzahim al-'Uqayli

When this poem is a love poem, it discloses everything about the lover, its poet; his inflamed love, his torment, destruction, and his actual madness sometimes. It uncovers especially his weakness and subservience toward his beloved. And it proclaims the beloved, all of her: her name, the name of her tribe, her address; it unveils her hair, her eyes, mouth, neck, hands, fingers, fingers nails, and often her breasts and waist and it often does not stop there. Let us read from this poem ascribed to Dawqala al-Manbiji:

I sigh for Da'd, and Da'd did not care
Save for the length of my affliction
White is she, her skin has clothed the splendour
Of beauty, so it is a skin for her skin
Adorning her cheeks, if she is unveiled,
Hair that is abundant braids, deep-black, curly
The face is, like morning, dawning
And the hair is, like night, black

The poem will continue its plundering course: the *forehead is smooth* and the *eyebrow is thin and long* and her *nose is adorned by pride* and her *teeth are well-arranged, as if their saliva is honey.* Then the poem goes below to the 'arms' of the beloved, to her 'fingertips', 'wrist', 'neck', 'breasts' and to every other part, not only from outside but also from inside, until her very heel bone. The poem, here, does not describe the beloved or write 'about' her, but rather it writes her, recreates and plunders her forever.

While searching for the 'nature' of the ancient Arabic poem, some researchers discovered, as if by magic, that this poem is 'descriptive', and they used this miraculous discovery as the best means to skim through the poem any time they wished. Apart from the fact that the ancient Arabic poem is not, essentially, a mere 'descriptive' poem, and that the question of the 'nature' of anything is not a literary but a philosophical matter, the definition of the ancient Arabic poem as 'descriptive' adds nothing to the 'philosophical' debate around the 'nature' of this poem. After all, everything made of language describes, even silence describes, because silence is the absence of language.

When this poem stops, with its poet, at the ruined home of the departed beloved, it becomes mad from sadness, it burns from memories, and it weeps over, and follows, everything there, big or small, low or high, because everything there is sacred and holy, from the memory of the beloved to the dung of the antelopes:

Stop to weep over the memory of a beloved and a home
At the end of the fine sand between Dakhul and Hawmal
Then between Tudih, and Miqrat
Its traces were not obliterated, for the wind blew them from south
and north
You could see the dung of the antelopes in its yards
And on its floors, as though grains of pepper

Imru' al-Qays

(*Dakhul, Hawmal, Tudih* and *Miqrat* are place names).

This poem speaks to everything around its poet: not only to the beloved's home, as we saw above, but to his love, his time, his sorrow, his pain, his night and day, and to his horse, his camel, the animals he encounters in the wilderness; it speaks to anything when it needs to speak. Of course, the poem knows that these things can not speak back in return:

I stopped to ask it [the ruined home], *but why do we ask*
Deaf, everlasting ones, whose speech doesn't come forth?

Labid ibn Rabi'a

But the painful fact that ruins do not speak does not hinder the poem from speaking and asking, because it needs to speak:

A valley like the onager's belly I passed through
Wherein the wolf howls like the one neglected that has a large
family
I said to him when he howled: our situation
Would be of little use had you not provided for yourself
Each of us, whenever he gets something, wastes it
And whoever acts like me and you will waste away

Imru' al-Qays

Because of its particular circumstances mentioned above, the ancient Arabic poem needed not only to speak but also to address its speech, even to the stones if there was nothing else but the stones, and even to the beast if there was nobody else but the beast. To speak, you need to address your speech. Iona, in Chekhov's *Misery*, after he failed to find anyone in the town willing to listen to his insufferable anguish at losing his son, spoke to his mare:

That's how it is, old girl… Kuzma Ionitch is gone… He said goodbye
to me… He went and died for no reason… Now, suppose you had a
little colt, and you were own mother to that little colt… And all at once
that same little colt went and died… You'd be sorry, wouldn't you?

18

This anguished question that Iona put to his mare can find its sad response in this extract from the famous ode of Labid ibn Rabi'a, who charged these lines, in fact his entire ode, with the tormented feeling of his weakness and exposure in the face of reality:

It is an antelope that lost her young one
Then her circling and mooing did not leave the gaps between
mountains
Searching for that white one covered in dust, wresting his torn off
limb
Ashen hunting wolves, whose eating doesn't stop
They came across her in an unguarded moment, then they hit
The arrows of death don't miss the target
She spent the night—continuous rain dropping
Watering the thickets—her tears continually flowing
While she is inside the hollow of a shrinking tree trunk, withdrawn
Near bases of dunes with sloping sand
Towering over her back a continuous rain
In a night whose clouds covered its stars

Walid Khazendar

The Traces of Song

One's life amongst mortals is nothing
More than lighting a flame in the wind

'Amr ibn Qami'a

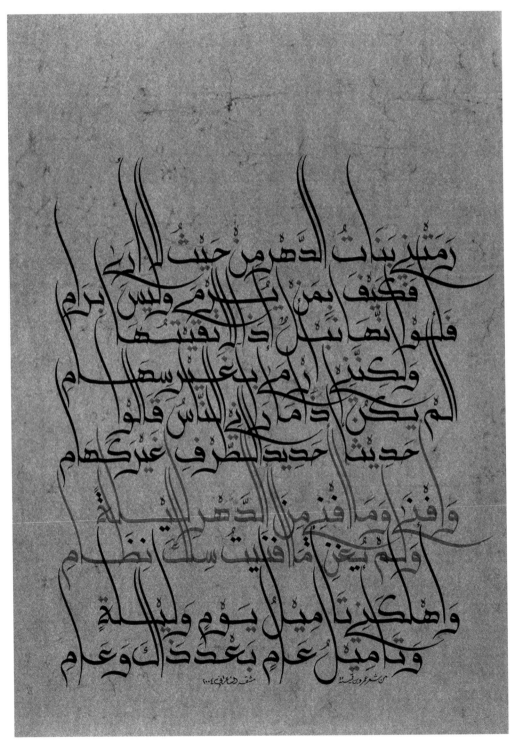

'Amr ibn Qami'a

24

They have shot me, the daughters of time, from where I do not see
And what of him who is shot at, and he's not shooting?
Had they been arrows I would have averted them
But I am being thrown at without darts.
If people saw me they would say: Wasn't he
Youthful, sharp-sighted, unflagging?
So I waste away and I don't waste a single night of time
Yet it did not yield, what I wasted, even a stringing-thread
And it has worn me out the hoping for a night and a day
And the hoping for a year, thereafter, and a year.

'Amr ibn Qami'a

Come clear, long night

Imru' al-Qays

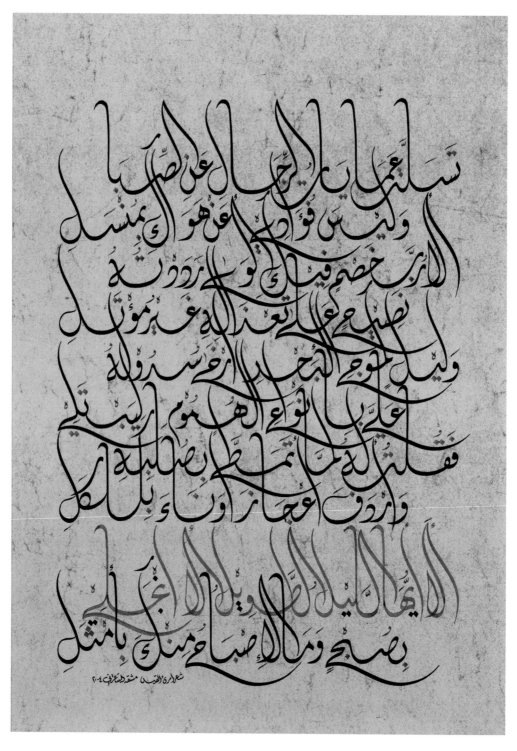

Imru' al-Qays

The follies of men have forgotten youth
But my heart does not forget your love.
Many a stubborn adversary over you whom I've repelled
Is sincere, and tireless in his blaming
And many a night, like the waves of the sea, lowered its curtains
Over me, with different griefs, to try me.
So I said, when it stretched its back
And followed with its rump, and weighed down heavily with its chest:
Come clear, long night
With a morning, while morning is no better than you.

Imru' al-Qays

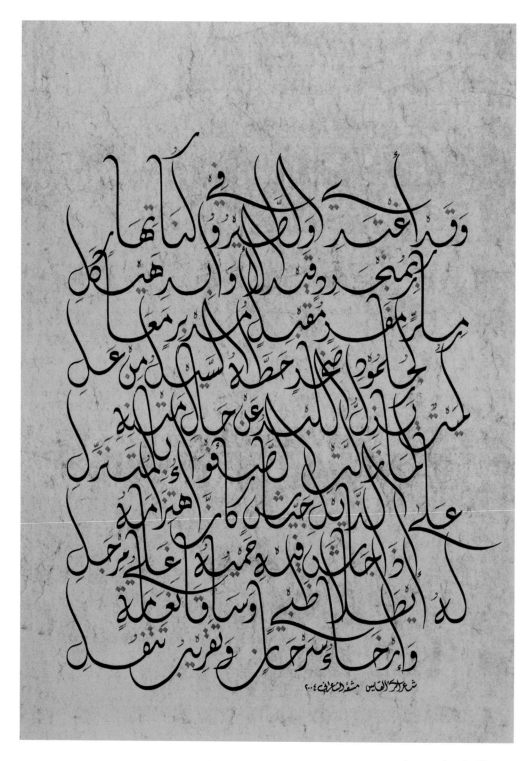

Imru' al-Qays

I may leave early in the morning, birds still in their shelters
On a speedy one, a shackle of wild animals, big-boned:
Attacking, fleeing, approaching, retreating, all in one
Like a huge rock dropped by the flood from above.
A bay, his mane slips down his back,
As the smooth stone makes the rain slip down.
Though thin he is excited as if his voice,
When his excitement surges, is a cauldron's boiling.
He has antelope flanks, and ostrich legs,
The gait of a wolf and the approach of a fox.

Imru' al-Qays

I'm a listener if one with insight answers

Abu Dhu'ayb al-Hudhali

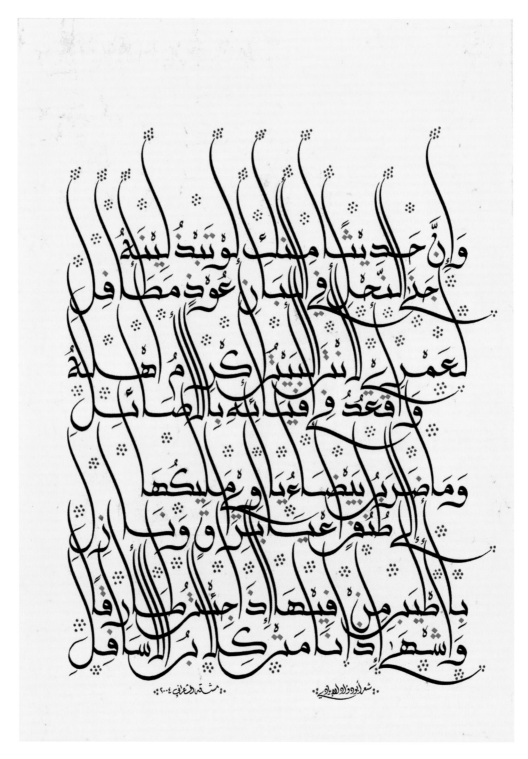

Abu Dhu'ayb al-Hudhali

34

Your speech, when you give generously,
Is the bees' harvest in the milk of a mother-camel:
"By my life, you are the home whose people I honour
And I sit in its shades, in the late afternoon".
The white honey—whose drone shelters
In eaves which defied whoever climbs and descends—
Is not more pleasant than her mouth, nor more delicious
If I come at night, when the dogs of the low valleys sleep.

Abu Dhu'ayb al-Hudhali

I see life as a treasure which lessens each night

Tarafa ibn al-'Abd

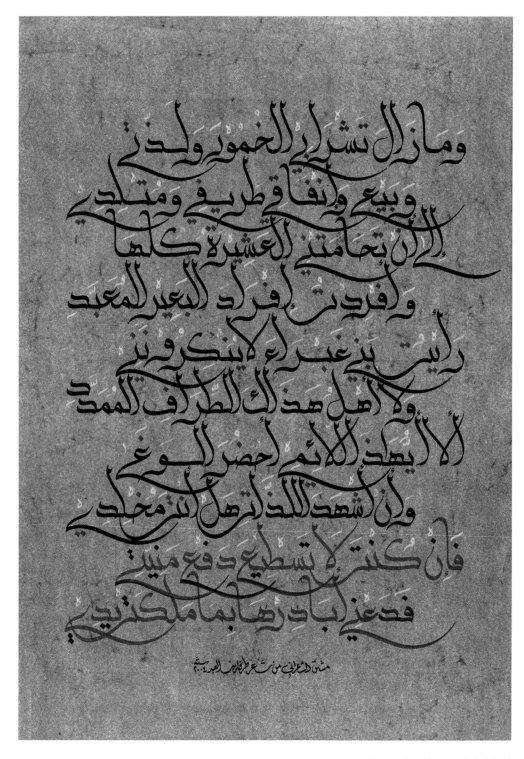

وما زال تشرابي الخمور ولذتي

وبيعي وإنفاقي طريفي ومتلدي

إلى أن تحامتني العشيرة كلها

وأفردت إفراد البعير المعبد

رأيت بني غبراء لا ينكرونني

ولا أهل هذاك الطراف الممدد

ألا أيهذا اللائم أحضر الوغى

وأن أشهد اللذات هل أنت مخلدي

فإن كنت لا تستطيع دفع منيتي

فدعني أبادرها بما ملكت يدي

مشتق هذا البيت من شعر طرفة بن العبد يقول

Tarafa ibn al-'Abd

My drinking and pleasure went on
And my buying and wasting new and old
Until the whole tribe had shunned me
And I was isolated like a tarred camel.
I found the poor didn't deny me
Nor the dwellers in spacious abodes
But you who blame me for joining in the clamour
And indulging in pleasure, are you making me immortal?
Since you can't drive away my death
Let me forestall it, by spending all that's in my hand.

Tarafa ibn al-'Abd

Man's life is a borrowed garment

al-Afwah al-Awdi

41

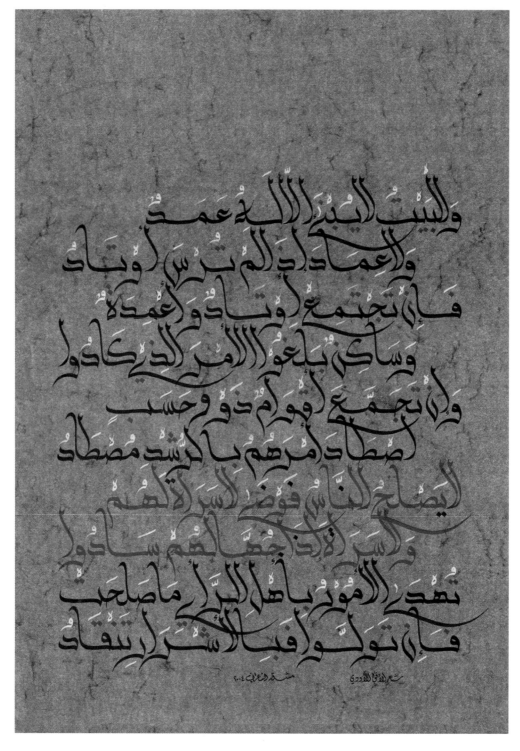

ولِلبَيتِ لابدَّ مِنَ الأرضِ يَعمُّ
وأعمادٍ إذا لم تُرسَ لا وتادٍ
فإن تَجمَّع أوتادٍ وأعمدةٍ
وسَاكِنٌ بلغوا الأمرَ الذي كادوا
ولا تَجمّعُ أقوامٌ ذَوُو وحَسَبٍ
لصطادٍ أمرِهم باركِ مصطادٍ
لِيُصلَحَ الناسُ فوضَى لا سَراةَ لهم
لا سراة إذا جُهّالُهم سادوا
تَهدي الأمورَ بِأهلِ الرأيِ ما صلحت
فإن تَولَّوا فبِالأشرارِ تنقادُ

مشقه ذو علي ١٠٤

شعر الأفوه الأودي

al-Afwah al-Awdi

42

A house can't be built unless with pillars
And there's no pillar if the bases aren't firm
And if bases, pillars and dwellers come together
They'll arrive at what they intended.
If good people come together
A hunter will hunt their affairs with integrity.
People don't thrive when chaotic, without notables
And there are no notables if the ignorant rule.
Matters are guided by the wise, as long as they are virtuous
So if they stray, they'll be guided by the evil.

al-Afwah al-Awdi

Be close to the gracious one
and strike fire with his brand

Hatim al-Ta'i

45

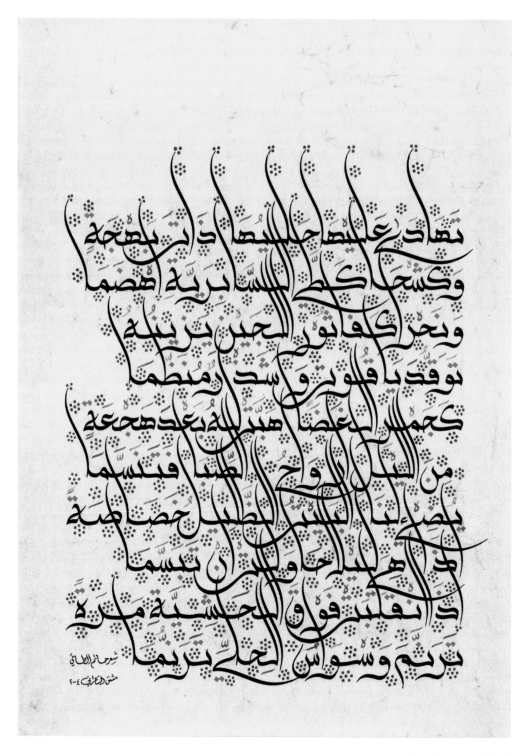

Hatim al-Ta'i

Sways, with her trinkets, she, endowed with splendour
With a waist like the fold of flimsy cloth, slim
And a neck like a cup of silver, adorning it
The blaze of the ruby and the strung beads
Like the ember of tamarisk, which, after a night's slumber
The breezes of youth wafted, then it flamed.
The house, shady with poverty, lights up for us
If, at night, she tries to smile.
If she turns over, once, on the mattress
The devil of jewels intones melodiously.

Hatim al-Ta'i

Nothing makes Man transparent like his distress

al-A'sha

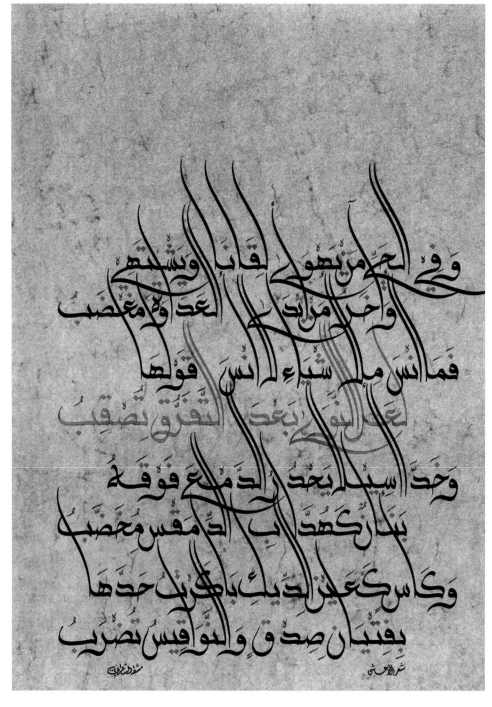

وفي الحي من يهوى هوانا ويشتهي
وآخر من آل المراد لنا عدو ولا نعصب

فما أنس من أشياء لا أنس قولها
لجارتها بعد ... التفرق تصقب

وخد أسيل يحدر الدمع فوقه
بنان كهداب الدمقس محضب

وكأس كعين الديك باكرت حدها
بفتيان صدق والنواقيس تضرب

al-A'sha

50

In the quarter are those who like us to meet and long for it,
And others who showed enmity and are angry.
If I forget some things, I don't forget her saying
"Perhaps distance after parting will be close"
Nor do I forget a smooth cheek bringing tears down, and over it
Fingertips, tinted like the fringe of damask
Nor a glass of wine like the cockerel's eye, whose sharpness I took early
With faithful friends, while bells were ringing.

al-A'sha

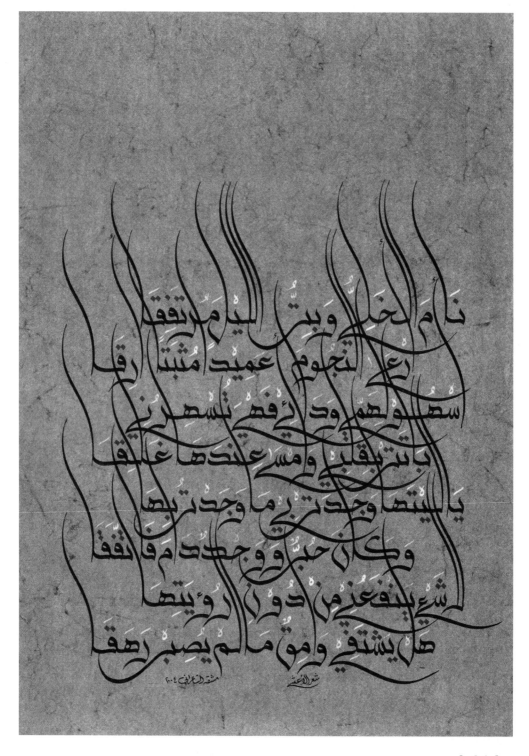

al-A'sha

52

The love-free slept and I spent the night propped on my elbow
Watching over the stars, love-sick, motionless, sleepless
Distracted by my grief and sickness, for she keeps me awake
She dwelt in my heart, and with her it became forfeit.
If only she longed for me as I long for her
And there was love and passion which endured then harmonised.
Nothing is of use to me without seeing her
Can the lover be cured without getting near?

al-A'sha

Resolution is useless without reflection

al-Nabigha al-Dhubyani

al-Nabigha al-Dhubyani

The veil dropped, she did not mean to drop it.
She picked it up and shielded herself from us with her hand
With a tender, tinted palm as if its fingers
Were tendrils, on their boughs, which did not dry
And with profuse, curly, coal-black hair, its growth
Like a vine that leant against the propped trellis.
She looked at you with a need she could not express
The look of the patient at the faces of visitors.

al-Nabigha al-Dhubyani

I see no cheerfulness in the evening-comers
If in the evening-comers there is no lover

Dahiya al-Hilaliya

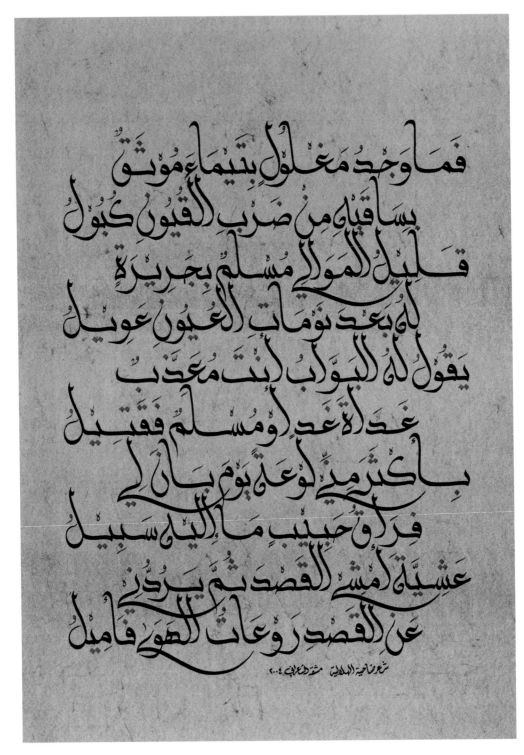

فَمَا وَجَدَ مَغْلُولٌ بِنِيماءٍ مُوثَقٌ
بِسَاقَيْهِ مِنْ ضَرْبِ الْقُيُونِ كَبُولُ

قَلِيلُ الْمَوَالِي مُسْلِمٌ بِجَرِيرَةٍ
لَهُ بَعْدَ نَوْمَاتِ الْعُيُونِ عَوِيلُ

يَقُولُ لَهُ الْبَوَّابُ أَنْتَ مُعَذَّبٌ
غَدًا لَا تَعُدْ أَوْ مُسْلِمٌ فَقَتِيلُ

بِأَكْثَرَ مِنِّي لَوْعَةً يَوْمَ بَانَ لِي
فِرَاقُ حَبِيبٍ مَا إِلَيْهِ سَبِيلُ

عَشِيَّةَ أَمْسِ الْقَصْدُ ثُمَّ يَرُدُّنِي
عَنِ الْقَصْدِ رَوْعَاتُ الْهَوَى فَأَمِيلُ

شعر ضاحية الهلالية   مشق الشربجي ٢٠٠٤

Dahiya al-Hilaliya

The grief of one chained in the wilderness—
Around his legs shackles forged by smiths
With few protectors, handed over for a crime
Wailing after the guards sleep
The doorkeeper saying to him: you'll be tortured
Tomorrow, or handed over and killed—
Is no more than my torment, the day it dawned on me
The leaving of a lover; no way to reach him
At evening when I walk resolutely, then am driven back
From resolution by the torments of love, so I turn.

Dahiya al-Hilaliya

Go for the virtuous, the graceful

'Abd Qays ibn Khufaf

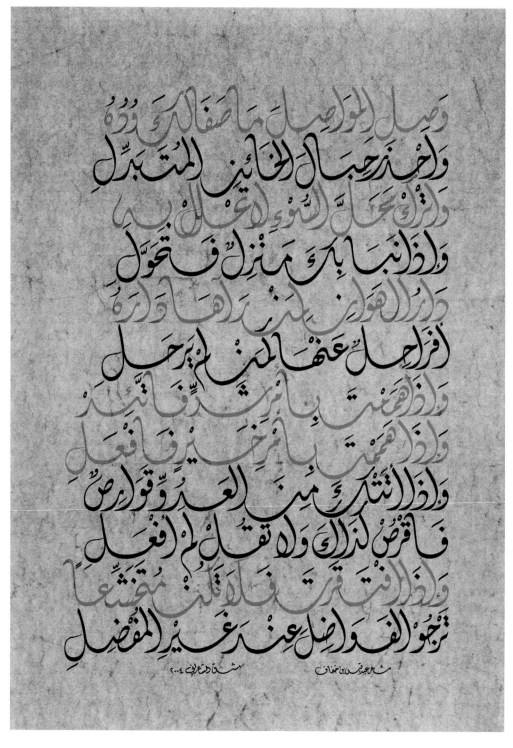

وَصِلْ الْمُوَاصِلَ مَا صَفَا لَكَ وُدُّهُ

وَاحْذَرْ حِبَالَ الْخَائِنِ الْمُتَبَدِّلِ

وَاتْرُكْ مَحَلَّ السُّوءِ لَا تَحْلُلْ بِهِ

وَإِذَا نَبَا بِكَ مَنْزِلٌ فَتَحَوَّلِ

دَارُ الْهَوَانِ لِمَنْ رَآهَا دَائِرَةٌ

أَفَرَاحِلٌ عَنْهَا أَمْ لَسْتَ بِرَاحِلِ

وَإِذَا هَمَمْتَ بِأَمْرٍ شَرٍّ فَائْتِهِ

وَإِذَا هَمَمْتَ بِأَمْرِ خَيْرٍ فَافْعَلِ

وَإِذَا أُثِرْتَ مِنَ الْعَدُوِّ وَقَوَارِصٍ

فَاقْرُصْ لِذَاكَ وَلَا تَقُلْ لَمْ أَفْعَلِ

وَإِذَا افْتَقَرْتَ فَلَا تُلِنْ مُتَخَشِّعًا

تَرْجُو الْفَوَاضِلَ عِنْدَ غَيْرِ الْمُفْضِلِ

مُشْقَ الْمَغْرِبِ ٢٠٠٤   شِعْرُ عَبْدِ قَيْسِ بْنِ خُفَافٍ

'Abd Qays ibn Khufaf

64

Keep the bond as long as the friendship is pure
And beware the traps of the traitor who changes.
Leave evil places, don't stay there
And when a home offends you, turn away.
The house of disgrace is for him who made it his:
Is he who left it like the one who didn't leave?
If you plan evil, wait awhile
And if you intend to do good, go ahead.
If an enemy's backbites get to you
Bite back like him, and don't say: "I didn't do it"
And if you become poor, don't be humble
Looking for favours from the favourless one.

'Abd Qays ibn Khufaf

The soul is one but care is spread

Ka'b ibn Zuhayr

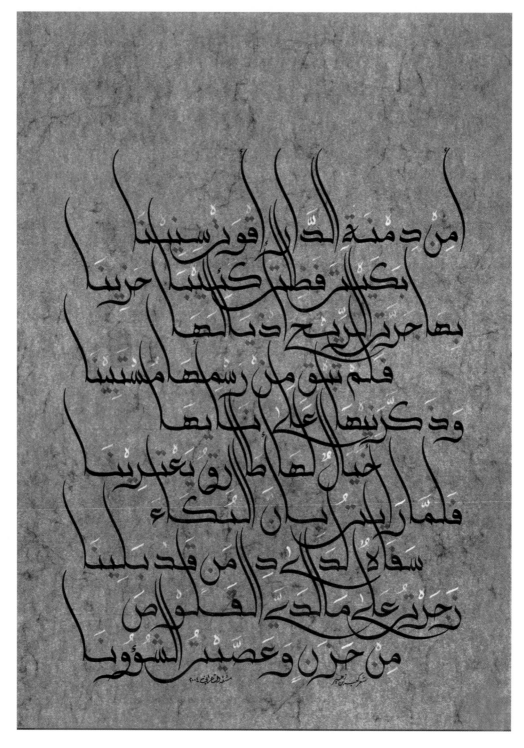

أمن رسم دمنة الدار أقوى بسينها

بعكاظ فطال كأسها حزينها

بها حرب الريح ديارها

فلم يبق من رسمها مسيسنا

وقد كنتها على أمايها

خيال الخطا أو بعثربنا

فلما رأيت أن لا شكاء

سفاه الدلحي من قد بيبنا

رحلت على ما حدى القلوص

من حزن وعصير السؤوبا

Ka'b ibn Zuhayr

68

Is it for the ruins of the home deserted for years
That you wept and remained depressed and sad?
The wind trailed its hems through them
It did not leave any of the traces clear.
And I was reminded of her, despite her remoteness
By her phantom, a night visitor that seizes me
But when I found it foolish
To weep over dilapidated ruins
I urged—despite all my sorrow—my mount on
And I resisted the tears.

Ka'b ibn Zuhayr

Dabi' ibn al-Harith

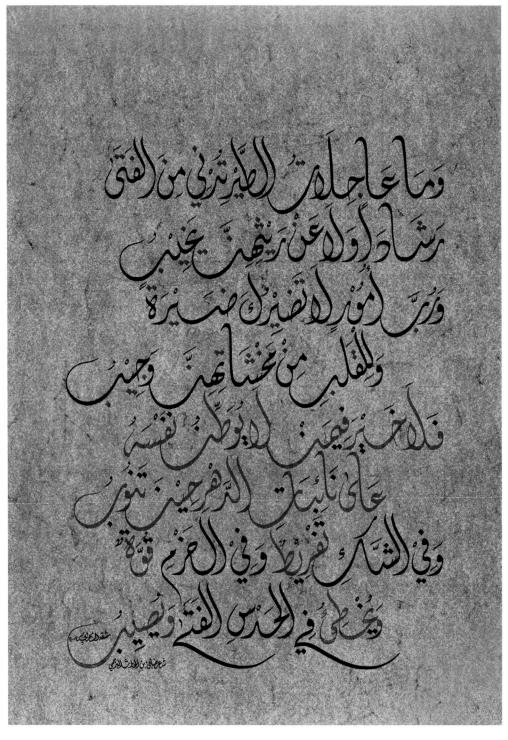

وَمَا عَاجِلَاتُ الطَّيْرِ تُدْنِي مِنَ الْفَتَى
رَشَادًا وَلَا عَنْ رَيْثِهِنَّ عَيْبُ

وَرُبَّ أُمُورٍ لَا تَضِيرُكَ ضَيْرَةٌ
وَلِلْقَلْبِ مِنْ مَخْشَاتِهِنَّ وَجِيبُ

فَلَا خَيْرَ فِيمَنْ لَا يُوَطِّنُ نَفْسَهُ
عَلَى نَائِبَاتِ الدَّهْرِ حِينَ تَنُوبُ

وَفِي الشَّكِّ تَفْرِيطٌ وَفِي الْحَزْمِ قُوَّةٌ
يُخَطِّئُ فِي الْحَدْسِ الْفَتَى وَيُصِيبُ

Dabi' ibn al-Harith

The hastening birds of fortune don't bring Man closer
To good sense, nor from their delay does he fail.
And there are many matters that won't bring you harm at all
Though the heart, for fear of them is pounding.
No good in him who does not hold himself firm
Against the blows of time when they strike.
In doubt lies shortcoming, in firmness strength
In guessing one may fail, or hit the mark.

Dabi' ibn al-Harith

Does the duration of days have an end?

Hassan ibn Thabit

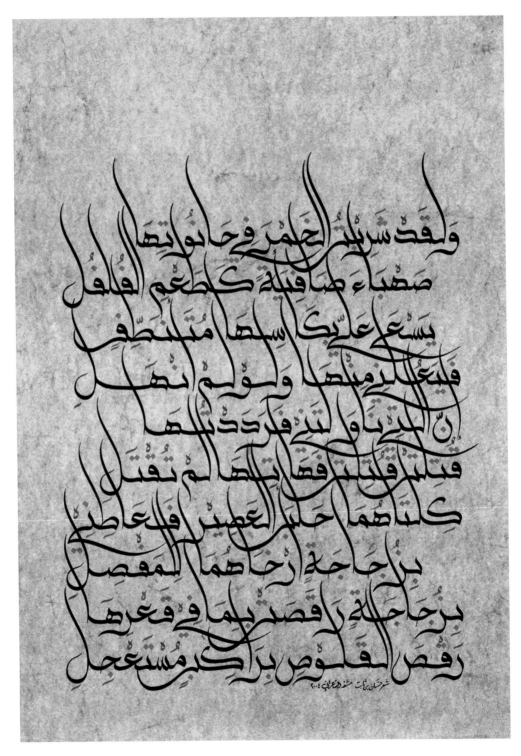

Hassan ibn Thabit

I have drunk the wine in its tavern
Reddish, pure, like the taste of pepper
Serving me with its glass an eardropped one
Giving me the second even if I did not drink the first:
That one you handed to me and I sent back
Has been killed—may you be killed—bring me the one still alive.
Both of them the extract of juice, give me then
A bottle more loosening to the joints
A bottle that surged with what lies within it
The surge of the long-legged mount with a hasty rider.

Hassan ibn Thabit

The heart has a devil's whisper
when the eye becomes bored

Qays ibn al-Mulawwah

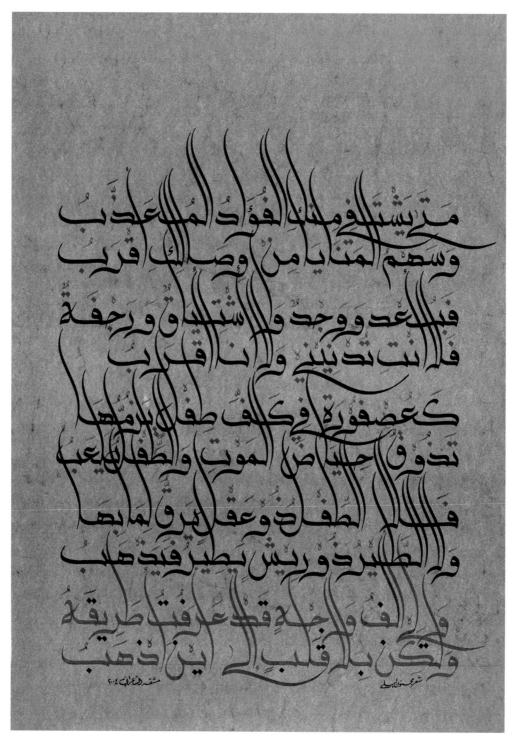

When will the tormented heart be cured of you
While the arrow of death is nearer to me than I to you.
Distance and love and longing and tremor
And you neither bring me near, nor I come close.
Like a sparrow in the palm of a child being squeezed
Tasting the water of death while the child plays.
Neither the child has the sense to feel for the bird
Nor the bird a feather to fly and to go.
I've a thousand directions whose ways I've known
But without a heart, where shall I go?

Qays ibn al-Mulawwah

She left me envying the beasts when I see
Two mates not frightened by the stampede

Abu Sakhr al-Hudhali

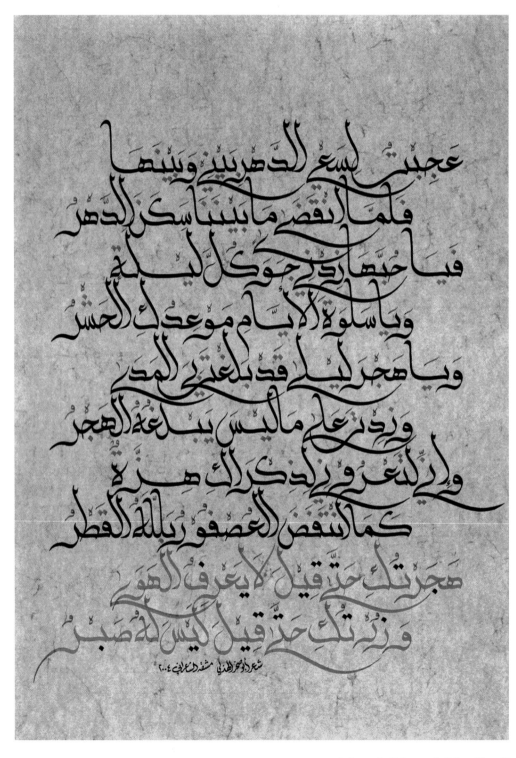

عجبت لسعي الدهر بيني وبينها فلما انقضى ما بيننا سكن الدهر

فيا حبذا الأيام إذ جو كل ليلة ويا سلوة الأيام موعدك الحشر

ويا هجر ليلى قد بلغت بي المدى وزدتني على ما ليس يبلغه الهجر

ولي بلعيني وبذكراك هزة كما انتفض العصفور بلله القطر

هجرتك حتى قيل لا يعرف الهوى وزرتك حتى قيل ليس له صبر

شعر أبو صخر الهذلي مشهد العربي ٢٠٠٤

Abu Sakhr al-Hudhali

I wonder at time's striving to come between me and her
And when what was between us ceased, time became calm.
My love for her, give me more passion every night
Consoling days, your time is the hereafter
And Layla's leaving, you took me so far
And went further than separation can reach.
A shiver seizes me when I remember you
As the sparrow trembled, when the rain made him wet.
I left you till they said: he knows nothing of love
And I visited you till they said: he has no patience.

Abu Sakhr al-Hudhali

My nearness to you is my sufficiency

Al-Ahwas al-Ansari

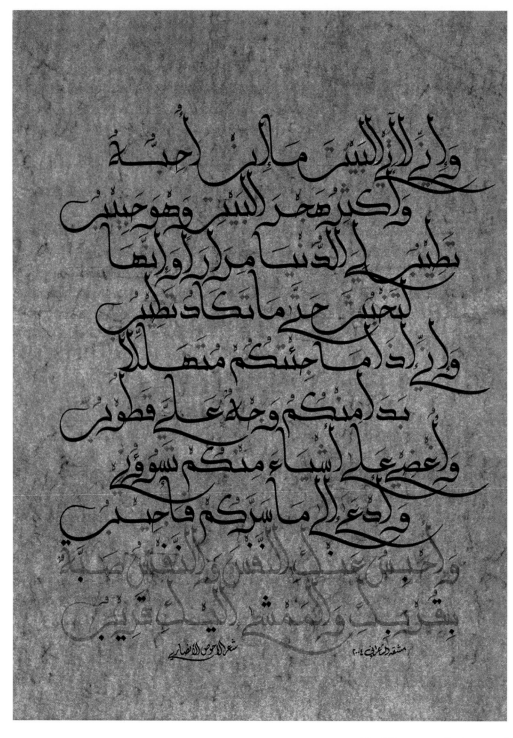

Al-Ahwas al-Ansari

I come to the house I don't like
And more often abandon the house which I love.
Life pleases me time and again
Yet offends till it scarcely pleases.
When I come to you, cheerfully
Your face seems sullen before me
While I overlook things about you that annoy me
And if I'm summoned to what pleases you, I respond.
I hold myself back from you though desiring
Your closeness, and the pathway towards you is near.

Al-Ahwas al-Ansari

I don't pursue the intimacy that is turning its back

Suwayd ibn Kura'

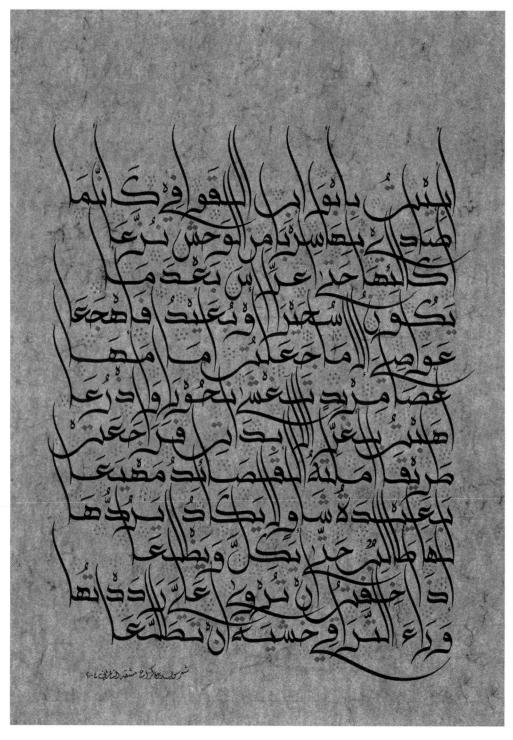

Suwayd ibn Kura'

92

I spend the night at the gateways of rhymes as if
I'm there cajoling a herd of wild animals, unruly.
I watch over them till I return late at night, when
The early dawn breaks, or a little later, then I rest a while.
Rebellious ones, unless I put across them
A stave restraining necks and forelegs.
I summoned the best of rhymes but they returned to
A broad pathway which poems have already paved.
They are beyond reach, a seeker can scarcely bring them in
Until he's exhausted and lame.
When I'm afraid they'll be quoted against me, I drive them back
Down my throat, for fear they might be heard.

Suwayd ibn Kura'

Night gathers tight around me
the trains of her love

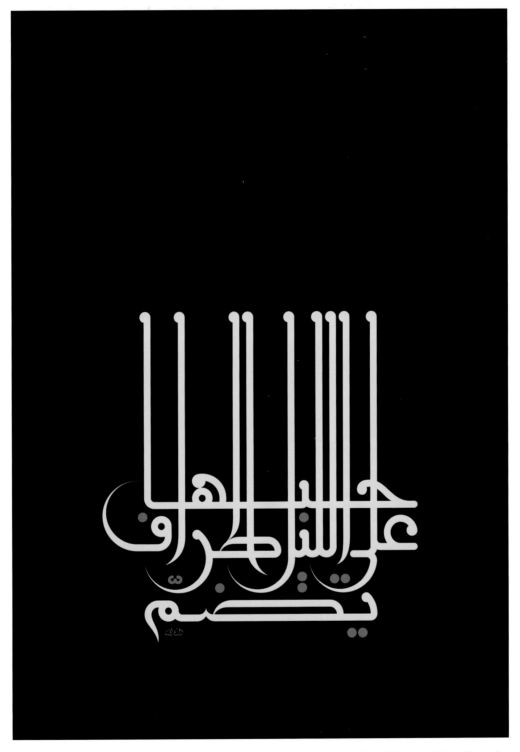

Nusayb ibn Rabah

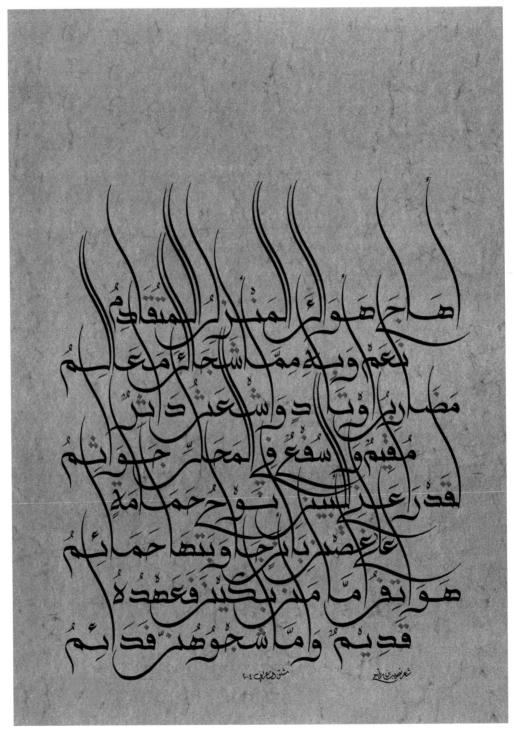

Nusayb ibn Rabah

96

Did it inflame your love that house getting older and older?
Yes, and in it are the traces of what made you grieve:
Tent peg mallets, a worn shaggy wedge
Still here, and black tripods, in place, still perching.
It has scared me a dove's lament for separation
On a Ben tree branch, and other doves answered
Cooing; the one they wept over
Is from an old time, but their grief is endless.

Nusayb ibn Rabah

As though the quivering of the lance is her gait

Dhu al-Rumma

Dhu al-Rumma

Passion doesn't bring back time past
Nor, from the remnants of the home, can one escape
At evening, when I have no way out save to be crazy
About picking up pebbles and writing on the sand.
I trace and erase the tracing then I retrace
With my hands, while crows in the house are perching
Past nights when to visit May was not remote
Nor was his heart scattered in love, seeking satisfaction.

Dhu al-Rumma

Ears don't hear except from the heart

Bashshar ibn Burd

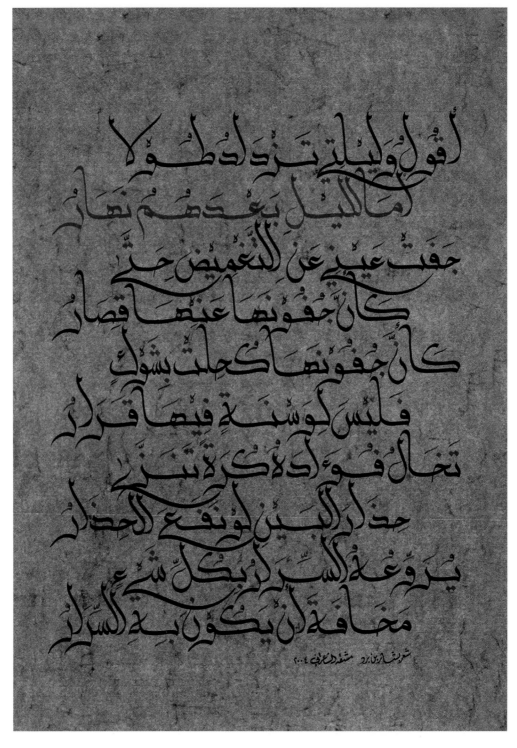

Bashshar ibn Burd

I say, as my night gets longer and longer:
Doesn't night, after them, have a day?
My eyes have shunned sleep
As if their eyelids fall short of them
As if their eyelids were kohled with thorns
So slumber has no rest in them.
You think his heart is a ball bouncing
Wary of separation, if wariness could be helpful.
It scares him the secret-telling about anything
Fearing the secret-telling is about him.

Bashshar ibn Burd

It's as though, since you left me,
I am absent

Abu Tammam

Abu Tammam

Perhaps I'll see you, so shall I see you with rapture
While living is tender and time still a boy?
They were years of love, their length made to be forgotten
By reminiscing distance, as if they were days.
Then days of separation set out, following
Passion with grief, as if they were years.
Then those years passed, so did their folk
As if they both were dreams.

Abu Tammam

Things become clear by their opposite

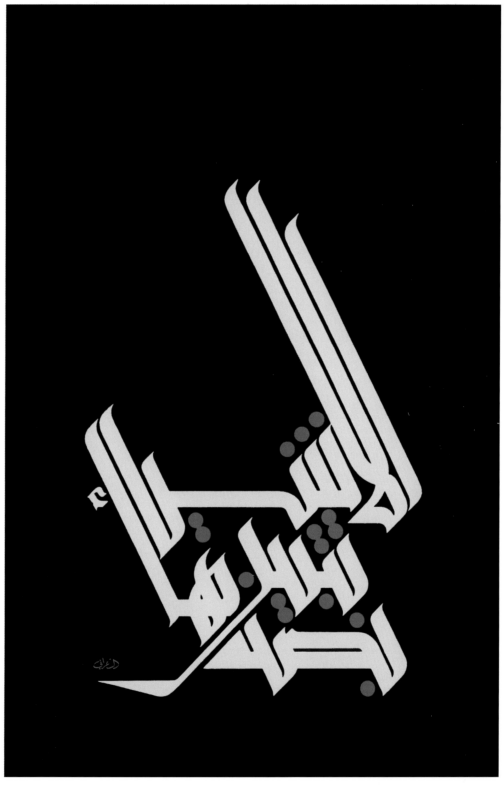

al-Mutanabbi

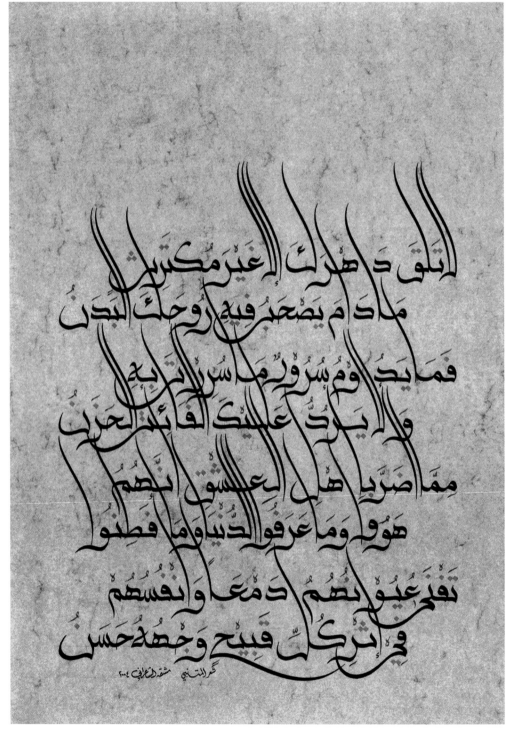

al-Mutanabbi

Don't meet your fate except indifferently
As long as your spirit is still with your body.
Pleasure doesn't last, however long it pleased you
And grief doesn't bring you back past time.
Part of what hurt those in love
Is that they loved, not knowing life, uncomprehending.
Their eyes are exhausted by tears while their souls
Follow every ugly person who has a beautiful face.

al-Mutanabbi

The roads to the heights aren't hidden

Abu Firas al-Hamdani

115

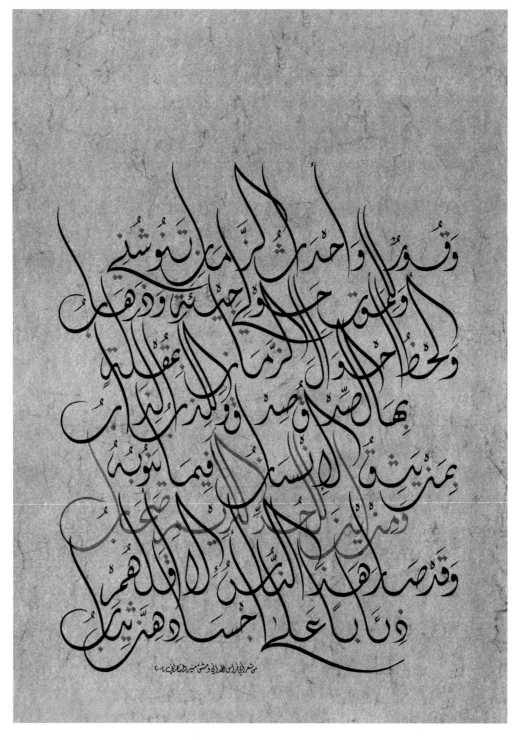

Abu Firas al-Hamdani

116

Composed, while the events of time skirmish with me
And death around me comes and goes.
I glance at time's conditions with an eye
Which sees truth is truth and lying is lying.
Whom can one trust with one's afflictions?
And where can the pure and noble find friends
When people, save a few,
Have become wolves wearing clothes?

Abu Firas al-Hamdani

The Arabic texts

لعمري لأنت البيت أكرم أهله
وأقعد في أفيائه بالأصائل
وما ضرب بيضاء يأوي مليكها
إلى طنف أعيا براق ونازل
بأطيب من فيها إذا جئت طارقا
وأشهى إذا نامت كلاب الأسافل
أبو ذؤيب الهذلي

Page 39

وما زال تشرابي الخمور ولذتي
وبيعي وإنفاقي طريفي ومتلدي
إلى أن تحامتني العشيرة كلها
وأفردت إفراد البعير المعبد
رأيت بني غبراء لا ينكرونني
ولا أهل هذاك الطراف الممدد
ألا أيهذا اللائمي أحضر الوغى
وأن أشهد اللذات هل أنت مخلدي
فإن كنت لا تستطيع دفع منيتي
فدعني أبادرها بما ملكت يدي
طرفة بن العبد

Page 43

والبيت لا يبنى إلا له عمد
ولا عماد إذا لم ترس أوتاد
فإن تجمع أوتاد وأعمدة
وساكن بلغوا الأمر الذي كادوا
وإن تجمع أقوام ذوو حسب
اصطاد أمرهم بالرشد مصطاد
لا يصلح الناس فوضى لا سراة لهم
ولا سراة إذا جهالهم سادوا
تهدى الأمور بأهل الرشد ما صلحت
فإن تولوا فبالأشرار تنقاد
الأفوه الأودي

Page 47

تهادى عليها حليها ذات بهجة
وكشحا كطي السابرية أهضما
ونحرا كفاثور اللجين يزينه
توقد ياقوت وشذر منظما
كجمر الغضا هبت له بعد هجعة
من الليل أرواح الصبا فتنسما
يضيء لنا البيت الظليل خصاصة
إذا هي ليلا حاولت أن تبسما

Page 25

رمتني بنات الدهر من حيث لا أرى
فكيف بمن يرمى وليس برام
فلو أنها نبل إذا لاتقيتها
ولكنني أرمى بغير سهام
إذا ما رآني الناس قالوا: ألم يكن
حديثا حديد الطرف غير كهام
وأفنى وما أفنى من الدهر ليلة
ولم يغن ما أفنيت سلك نظام
وأهلكني تأميل يوم وليلة
وتأميل عام بعد ذاك وعام
عمرو بن قميئة

Page 29

تسلت عمايات الرجال عن الصبا
وليس فؤادي عن هواك بمنسل
ألا رب خصم فيك ألوى رددته
نصيح على تعذاله غير مؤتل
وليل كموج البحر أرخى سدوله
علي بأنواع الهموم ليبتلي
فقلت له لما تمطى بصلبه
وأردف أعجازا وناء بكلكل
ألا أيها الليل الطويل ألا انجلي
بصبح وما الإصباح منك بأمثل
امرؤ القيس

Page 31

وقد اغتدي والطير في وكناتها
بمنجرد قيد الأوابد هيكل
مكر مفر مقبل مدبر معا
كجلمود صخر حطه السيل من عل
كميت يزل اللبد عن حال متنه
كما زلت الصفواء بالمتنزل
على الذبل جياش كأن اهتزامه
إذا جاش فيه حميه غلي مرجل
له أيطلا ظبي وساقا نعامة
وإرخاء سرحان وتقريب تتفل
امرؤ القيس

Page 35

وإن حديثا منك لو تبذلينه
جنى النحل في ألبان عوذ مطافل

119

إذا انقلبت فوق الحشية مرة

ترنم وسواس الحلي ترنما

حاتم الطائي

Page 51

وفي الحي من يهوى لقانا ويشتهي

وآخر من أبدى العداوة مغضب

فما أنس ملأشياء لا أنس قولها

لعل النوى بعد التفرق تصقب

وخدا أسيلا يحدر الدمع فوقه

بنان كهداب الدمقس مخضب

وكأس كعين الديك باكرت حدها

بفتيان صدق والنواقيس تضرب

الأعشى

Page 53

نام الخلي وبت الليل مرتفقا

أرعى النجوم عميدا مثبتا أرقا

أسهو لهمي ودائي فهي تسهرني

باتت بقلبي وأمسى عندها غلقا

ياليتها وجدت بي ما وجدت بها

وكان حب ووجد دام فاتفقا

لا شيء ينفعني من دون رؤيتها

هل يشتفي وامق مالم يصب رهقا

الأعشى

Page 57

سقط النصيف ولم ترد إسقاطه

فتناولته واتقتنا باليد

بمخضب رخص كأن بنانه

عنم على أغصانه لم يعقد

وبفاحم رجل أثيث نبته

كالكرم مال على الدعام المسند

نظرت إليك بحاجة لم تقضها

نظر السقيم إلى وجوه العود

النابغة الذبياني

Page 61

فما وجد مغلول بتيماء موثق

بساقيه من ضرب القيون كبول

قليل الموالي مسلم بجريرة

له بعد نومات العيون عويل

يقول له البواب أنت معذب

غداة غد أومسلم فقتيل

بأكثر مني لوعة يوم بان لي

فراق حبيب ما إليه سبيل

عشية أمشي القصد ثم يردني

عن القصد روعات الهوى فأميل

ضاحية الهلالية

Page 65

وصل المواصل ما صفا لك وده

واحذر حبال الخائن المتبدل

واترك محل السوء لا تحلل به

وإذا نبا بك منزل فتحول

دار الهوان لمن رآها داره

أفراحل عنها كمن لم يرحل

وإذا هممت بأمر شر فاتئد

وإذا هممت بأمر خير فافعل

وإذا أتتك من العدو قوارص

فاقرص كذاك ولا تقل لم أفعل

وإذا افتقرت فلا تكن متخشعا

ترجو الفواضل عند غير المفضل

عبد قيس بن خفاف

Page 69

أمن دمنة الدار أقوت سنينا

بكيت فظلت كئيبا حزينا

بها جرت الريح أذيالها

فلم تبق من رسمها مستبينا

وذكرنيها على نأيها

خيال لها طارق يعترينا

فلما رأيت بأن البكاء

سفاه لدى دمن قد بلينا

زجرت على ما لدي القلوص

من حزن وعصيت الشؤونا

كعب بن زهير

Page 73

وما عاجلات الطير تدني من الفتى

رشادا ولا عن ريثهن يخيب

ورب أمور لا تضيرك ضيرة

وللقلب من مخشاتهن وجيب

فلا خير فيمن لا يوطن نفسه

على نائبات الدهر حين تنوب

وفي الشك تفريط وفي الحزم قوة

120

ويخطئ في الحدس الفتى ويصيب

ضابئ بن الحارث

Page 77

ولقد شربت الخمر في حانوتها
صهباء صافية كطعم الفلفل
يسعى علي بكأسها متنطف
فيعلني منها ولو لم أنهل
إن التي ناولتني فرددتها
قتلت قتلت فهاتها لم تقتل
كلتاهما حلب العصير فعاطني
بزجاجة أرخاها للمفصل
بزجاجة رقصت بما في قعرها
رقص القلوص براكب مستعجل

حسان بن ثابت

Page 81

متى يشتفي منك الفؤاد المعذب
وسهم المنايا من وصالك أقرب
فبعد ووجد واشتياق ورجفة
فلا أنت تدنيني ولا أنا أقرب
كعصفورة في كف طفل يزمها
تذوق حياض الموت والطفل يلعب
فلا الطفل ذو عقل لما بها
ولا الطير ذو ريش يطير فيذهب
ولي ألف وجه قد عرفت طريقه
ولكن بلا قلب إلى أين أذهب

قيس بن الملوح

Page 85

عجبت لسعي الدهر بيني وبينها
فلما انقضى ما بيننا سكن الدهر
فيا حبها زدني جوى كل ليلة
ويا سلوة الأيام موعدك الحشر
ويا هجر ليلى قد بلغت بي المدى
وزدت على ما ليس يبلغه الهجر
وإني لتعروني لذكراك هزة
كما انتفض العصفور بلله القطر
هجرتك حتى قيل لا يعرف الهوى
وزرتك حتى قيل ليس له صبر

أبو صخر الهذلي

Page 89

وإني لآتي البيت ما إن أحبه

وأكثر هجر البيت وهو حبيب
تطيب لي الدنيا مرارا وإنها
لتخبث حتى ما تكاد تطيب
وإني إذا ما جئتكم متهللا
بدا منكم وجه علي قطوبوأغضي على
أشياء منكم تسوءني
وأدعى إلى ما سركم فأجيب
وأحبس عنك النفس والنفس صبة
بقربك والممشى إليك قريب

الأحوص الأنصاري

Page 93

أبيت بأبواب القوافي كأنما
أصادي بها سربا من الوحش نزعا
أكالئها حتى أعرس بعدما
يكون سحير أو بعيد فأهجعا
عواصي إلا ما جعلت أمامها
عصا مربد تغشى نحورا وأذرعا
أهبت بغر الآبدات فراجعت
طريقا أملته القصائد مهيعا
بعيدة شأو لا يكاد يردها
لها طالب حتى يكل ويظلعا
إذا خفت أن تروى علي رددتها
وراء التراقي خشية أن تطلعا

سويد بن كراع

Page 97

هاج هواك المنزل المتقادم
نعم وبه مما شجاك معالم
مضارب أوتاد وأشعث داثر
مقيم وسفع في المحل جواثم
لقد راعني للبين نوح حمامة
على غصن بان جاوبتها حمائم
هواتف أما من بكين فعهده
قديم وأما شجوهن فدائم

نصيب بن رباح

Page 101

وما يرجع الوجد الزمان الذي مضى
ولا للفتى من دمنة الدار مجزع
عشية ما لي حيلة غير أنني
بلقط الحصى والخط في الترب مولع
أخط وأمحو الخط ثم أعيده
بكفي والغربان في الدار وقع

ثم انقضت تلك السنون وأهلها
فكأنها وكأنهم أحلام

أبو تمام

Page 113

لا تلق دهرك إلا غير مكترث
ما دام يصحب فيه روحك البدن
فما يدوم سرور ما سررت به
ولا يرد عليك الفائت الحزن
مما أضر بأهل العشق أنهم
هووا وما عرفوا الدنيا وما فطنوا
تفنى عيونهم دمعا وأنفسهم
في إثر كل قبيح وجهه حسن

المتنبي

Page 117

وقور وأحداث الزمان تنوشني
وللموت حولي جيئة وذهاب
وألحظ أحوال الزمان بمقلة
بها الصدق صدق والكذاب كذاب
بمن يثق الإنسان فيما ينوبه
ومن أين للحر الكريم صحاب
وقد صار هذا الناس إلا أقلهم
ذئابا على أجسادهن ثياب

أبو فراس الحمداني

ليالي لا مي بعيد مزارها
ولا قلبه شتى الهوى متشبع

ذو الرمة

Page 105

أقول وليلتي تزداد طولا
أما لليل بعدهم نهار
جفت عيني عن التغميض حتى
كأن جفونها عنها قصار
كأن جفونها كحلت بشوك
فليس لوسنة فيها قرار
تخال فؤاده كرة تنزى
حذار البين لو نفع الحذار
يروعه السرار بكل شيء
مخافة أن يكون به السرار

بشار بن برد

Page 109

ولقد أراك فهل أراك بغبطة
والعيش غض والزمان غلام
أعوام وصل كان ينسي طولها
ذكر النوى فكأنها أيام
ثم انبرت أيام هجر أردفت
بجوى أسى فكأنها أعوام

The Arabic quotations

Notes

'Abd Qays ibn Khufaf
(6th cent. A.D.)

He was the poet, and a chief, of his tribe. His poems were included in ancient Arabic anthologies of the best of early Arabic poetry. The extract which appears in this book is from one of his few poems that have come down to us. He addressed this poem to his son, and it is considered to be the earliest text we have about lived experience and the morals and spiritual education of ancient times in the Arabian peninsula.

Abu Dhu'ayb al-Hudhali
(6th cent. A.D.)

A poet and a knight. The ancient Arabic references say that the poet Hassan ibn Thabit (also included in this book) described him as "the most important poet of his time". His language is eloquent and his poetry full of realistic scenes and sensual, concrete images. The beloved in his amatory poems is a vital presence and usually has something to say in the poem. The ancient sources describe him as a brave knight, and a handsome man and sensitive lover. Amongst the most beautiful and famous of his long poems is an elegy for his five sons who died from the plague, and a love poem from which the extract in this book is taken.

Abu Firas al-Hamdani
(10th cent. A.D.)

A poet, knight, and prince. His poetry is at once simple and eloquent, pleasant and grand, tender and sound. His poetry was collected and edited while he was still alive, with a commentary said to have been written by the poet himself. It includes short erotic poems, most of them not more than six verses long.

Abu Sakhr al-Hudhali
(7th cent. A.D.)

He is renowned for his passion and love poetry. The traces of artifice in his poetry are few, and his sentiments are expressed in a clear simple language. Only a few of his poems have been preserved. His verses included in this book are from a poem considered by the ancient Arab critics as the "most passionate of Arabic poetry".

Abu Tammam
(9th cent. A.D.)

His poetry marks one of the most important poetic moments in ancient Arabic poetry. Some of his verses are considered to be a crucial turning point in this poetry from concrete image to conceptual metaphor. His style was a source of controversy from the beginning of his writing and this continued for many centuries. Many ancient Arab critics have debated his merits. He compiled a famous poetry anthology called *The Book of Valour*, which contained what, in his view, was the best of Arabic poetry up to his time.

al-A'sha
(6th cent. A.D.)

Ancient Arabic sources refer to

him as "the master of poets" of the pre-Islamic period. He has been called "the castanet player of the Arabs" because he used to sing his poetry. In addition to his panegyrics, he contributed to most of the themes of ancient poetry. He is the most famous wine poet and his love poetry is very daring, both socially and artistically. Early sources claim that after his death the "young men would drink to his company, treating his tomb as one of them, and when the glass of wine reached it, they poured the wine over it."

al-Afwah al-Awdi
(6th cent. A.D.)

He was the poet of his tribe, and its chief and commander. He was known as a wise man, as his prose testifies: "Experience is knowledge, and good manners are a support, and to desist from these is harmful. Let your companions be those who are generous and encourage generosity; avoid the company of devils, for rancour will follow….."

al-Ahwas al-Ansari
(7th cent. A.D.)

The language of his poetry was fluent, with well chosen words. Glamour and simplicity were the dominant traits of his poetry. Apart from his very tender amatory poems he wrote panegyrics. Ancient Arab critics who refer to him as an important poet, also speak about "his base acts … he used to rhapsodize about the women of the nobles of the city of Medina and spread this amongst people".

al-Mutanabbi
(10th cent. A.D.)
He is the most famous poet in ancient Arabic poetry. Besides being the poet of kings and princes, he was the most popular poet of his time and even of modern times. His poetry is imaginative, metaphorical and tenacious, and it has inspired many commentaries and critical works, both in his time and even today. The best of his poetry is of the wisdom genre and contains lessons of life and love. The sources give the following account of how he was killed for "a verse of poetry", when his enemies attacked him while he was travelling in the desert: "After he fought fiercely, he wanted to retreat, then his servant said to him: 'Where is your verse:

Horses and night and wilderness know me
And stabbing and fencing, and paper and pen?'

Then he answered: 'You've killed me, God kill you!' And he continued to fight till he was killed."

al-Nabigha al-Dhubyani
(6th cent. A.D.)

One of the great court poets in ancient Arabic literature. His poetry is of a high artistic style characterised by powerful imagination and sentimentality. His style is devoid of affectation and tautology. The sources say that he used to sit under "a red dome of leather in Ukaz market, and the poets used to come to show their poetry to him."

'Amr ibn Qami'a
(5th-6th cent. A.D.)

One of the earliest poets whose works have survived. His poems are the most ancient in Arabic poetry. He was a member of a family of poets. His poetry is unaffected and mostly sad, focusing on the harshness of reality.

Bashshar ibn Burd
(8th cent. A.D.)

He was a master of erotic poems and panegyric and his satires were much feared. His bad temper and sharp tongue earned him a reputation as one whose displeasure was to be avoided. His impudent poetry and his parodic poems were extremely popular and often condemned. He was blind from birth and said to have been exceptionally ugly but, despite this, he was widely sought after both by women and by important officials. His poems were collected very late, and they were known principally through anthologies. Many of the critics considered him the first of the modern poets of his time. He had a great influence on the subsequent generation of poets.

Dabi' ibn al-Harith
(7th cent. A.D.)

The sources say little about his life. What survived of his poetry is a very few poems, but they show a coherent and fluent personal language, and one who was very much his own man.

Dahiya al- Hilaliya
(Between 5th and 6th cent. A.D.)

Early poetess, about whom nothing is known. Her few poems that have reached us are all love poems. Her style is artistic, full of images, emotional and revealing.

Dhu al-Rumma
(7th cent. A.D.)
His poems reflect and represent the language and style of early Arabic poetry from the pre-Islamic period. His erotic poetry has the typical features of platonic love poetry. He was the leader of the grammarians of his time and was often called upon to determine the authenticity of early poems.

Hassan ibn Thabit
(7th cent. A.D.)

"The most poetic of the town poets", as sources describe him. His love poetry is emotional and sentimental, and generally he was a tender-hearted man who hated violence. Ancient references recount how "one day he climbed a hill and shouted: 'You men, you men!' People gathered around him and asked him: 'What is the matter with you'? He said: 'Listen!' And then he said:

*Sleep was prevented, at evening, by grief
And by a phantom, while the stars were sinking*

When he finished the poem people said: 'Is it for this that you gathered us together?' He said: 'If this had remained inside me it would have killed me'." In the Islamic period he was the most important of those poets who associated themselves with the Prophet Muhammad.

Hatim al-Ta'i
(6th cent. A.D.)

A poet and knight. With a fluent language and sensual images and metaphors, his poems are concerned with his home and his family, his neighbours and guests. His poetry was considered the embodiment of ancient Arabic virtues. The poems attributed to him are mostly short and glorify honesty, modesty, and hospitality.

Imru' al-Qays
(6th cent. A.D.)

The ancient Arabic critics describe him as the creator of the classical form of the ancient poem. His poetry is marked by the ingenuity of his images and metaphors. His ode, included in the famous and very old anthology of early Arabic poetry called *The Odes*, aroused the most interest. Without exception, he is the most famous early Arab poet, both for his poetry and his life story: as a child he had lived at the court of his father, the last king of Kinda, but his passion for poetry, and especially erotic poetry, led to his being expelled from his father's house. He began to lead the life of a carefree vagabond, dividing his time between hunting, drinking and song. It was during a drinking session that he received the news that his father had been assassinated. From then on, his only aim was to avenge his father.

Ka'b ibn Zuhayr
(7th cent. A.D.)

His poetry displays much originality especially in its images of desert journeys and animals. Most of his poems are short and flowing with easy and clear phrases, focusing mostly on one motif or subject. He is the son of Zuhayr ibn Abi Sulma, one of the most famous early poets.

Nusayb ibn Rabah
(7th cent. A.D.)

His poems are relatively short and direct. His imagery, however, is rich and condensed. In love poetry he is the first to treat the motif of the grieving dove. His love poetry has the tone of platonic love with a strong sense of place.

Qays ibn al-Mulawwah
(7th cent. A.D.)

His poetry and love for Layla are widely known in Arabic literature and Arab societies, ancient and modern. His love story with Layla is the Arabic equivalent of the story of "Romeo and Juliet". As the story goes his love had developed in his childhood years, but Layla's parents, resentful of his behaviour, married her to someone else. This intensified his passion, which caused him to roam about in search of relief and led him to madness. He lived and died in the wilderness, far from human habitation, accepting only wild beasts for company. During his agony, poetic inspiration never failed him whenever he remembered Layla, and his passion for her often mingles with the longing for his homeland.

Suwayd ibn Kura'
(7th cent. A.D.)

A poet and a knight. His poetry is well-formed and balanced with quiet and studied images. The sources say he used to revise his poetry long before reciting it. The extract in this book is from a famous long poem, in which he gives his view of poetry writing.

Tarafa ibn al-'Abd
(6th cent. A.D.)

Ancient Arab critics ranked him in a class just below Imru'

al-Qays, and thought him a skilled poet who composed long poems at a high artistic level. His long poem included in *The Odes* is characterised by a vast imagination and original, concrete comparisons that burst forth throughout the poem. In addition to his ode he has many fine poems, long and short. He was a rebellious poet, both against his tribe and against the social conventions of his time.

Visiting Arts

Pembox Trust   •   **Seven Pillars of Wisdom Trust**